Twenty to Make

Sugar Wobblies

Georgie God

Search Press

First published in Great Britain 2013

Search Press Limited
Wellwood, North Farm Road,
Tunbridge Wells, Kent TN2 3DR

Text copyright © Georgie Godbold 2013

Photographs by Debbie Patterson at
Search Press Studios

Photographs and design copyright
© Search Press Ltd 2013

Print ISBN: 978-1-84448-832-2
EPUB ISBN: 978-1-78126-049-4
Mobi ISBN: 978-1-78126-103-3
PDF ISBN: 978-1-78126-157-6

The Publishers and author can accept no
responsibility for any consequences arising
from the information, advice or instructions
given in this publication.

Suppliers
If you have difficulty in obtaining any of the
materials and equipment mentioned in this
book, then please visit the Search Press website
for details of suppliers: www.searchpress.com

Printed in Malaysia

Dedication
*This book is dedicated to Chris, my very
patient and understanding husband; and
to my family, especially my grandchildren
Charlie and Amelia.
A very big thank you to my friend
Beryl for all her help and support and
to everyone who has encouraged me
to write this book.
To say thank you to you all, I have
named each of my sugar wobblies
after one of you!*

Contents

Introduction

These cute little 'sugar wobblies' are non-edible sugarcraft decorations that can be placed on a cake or presented as a gift, providing a memorable keepsake that will last for years to come.

These characters are all designed using pipe cleaners for parts such as the arms, legs and tails, which means that they wobble gently when touched – hence their name. Pipe cleaners are used because they can easily be bent into shape and, more importantly, they do not fall off!

Children love to make them because they are easy to assemble and decorate. More advanced sugar crafters will find satisfaction, once the basic skills have been mastered, in using their own ideas to add personal touches to create a sugar wobbly appropriate for each individual recipient.

Have fun and good luck.

Basic shapes

The wobblies in this book are made from common parts and shapes. This page explains how to make these basic parts, before you start following the instructions for each individual wobbly.

Bodies:

All wobbly bodies are the same size.

1 Roll 45g (1½oz) of modelling paste into a ball.

2 Shape the paste into a cone 6.5cm (2½in) tall.

3 Insert an 8cm (3¼in) cocktail stick through the middle of the cone to the base for support. The top of the cocktail stick will support the head. Make two holes in the front for the legs to fit in.

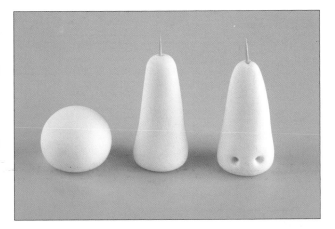

Heads:

1 Roll 20g (⅔oz) of modelling paste into a smooth ball. Make a small hole in the middle of the face ready for the nose.

2 Make a small round-ended cone of paste for the nose and insert it into the hole using a small amount of sugar glue.

3 Use a smiley tool or drinking straw to make the mouth.

4 Make two holes for the eyes and leave to dry.

Eyes:

1 These are made using stamens (see opposite page). Insert them into the head and leave to dry. If you cannot obtain stamens, you can use two very small balls of white paste.

2 Use a fine black fibre-tip pen to mark the pupils.

Tools and materials

Tools:

You will need these basic tools for nearly all the projects in this book: a **pointed tool**, a **smiley tool** or **drinking straw**, **paintbrushes** for dusting paste or attaching pieces together, a **texture frilling tool**, and a **ball tool**. Some of the tools are double-ended – the pointed tool has one pointed and one rounded end, for example.

A **non-stick work board** makes it easier to roll out the paste without it moving. Place a **non-slip mat** underneath to prevent your board from moving.

Small non-stick rolling pin This is used for rolling out your paste.

Small pair of scissors These are used to cut paste or ribbons.

Use a small thin **palette knife** to release paste from your board.

Cutters, made of plastic or metal, come in various shapes such as ovals, circles or hearts.

Small **blossom cutters** are easy to use flower-shaped cutters that come in many sizes.

A **Garrett frill cutter** can make large circle frills.

Cocktail sticks are used to support the bodies and for texturing.

Mini digital scales are ideal for weighing out small amounts of paste.

Pipe cleaners, also called chenille sticks, can be obtained in various colours from craft shops.

Small pieces of **foam** help support sugar items whilst they are drying.

Stamens are round beads attached to a stick for decorating blossoms. These are used for eyes.

For **food colourings**, I like to use edible art dusting colours such as those from Edable Art, or paste food colours.

Icing tubes are used for making circles, buttons or dots, as on the ladybird and dinosaur.

Small **wire cutters** are used to cut the cocktail sticks and pipe cleaners to the required length.

To make very thin strands of sugarpaste for hair, use a **clay gun** or **sieve**.

Confectioner's glaze will allow you to give a shiny finish to painted noses.

Materials:

Modelling paste can be purchased from sugarcraft shops or online cake decorating suppliers. It can also be made by kneading together equal parts of sugarpaste with flower or gum paste. Wrap sugarpaste tightly in freezer bags to prevent it from drying out between uses.

Sugar glue is made by slowly warming 15g (½oz) sugarpaste and 15g (½oz) water in the microwave until it boils. When cool it is ready for use. Sugar glue keeps well in a small screw top jar.

Icing sugar is used when rolling out your paste.

White fat stops the paste sticking to the board when rolling out.

Lion

Materials:

120g (4¼oz) brown or chocolate modelling paste

Small amounts of cream, black and blue modelling paste

Small amount of tangerine flower paste/gum paste

One pipe cleaner, stripy if possible

Two large white stamens

Cocktail stick

Tools:

Basic tools (see page 7)

Fine black fibre-tip pen

Cutters: 6cm (2⅜in) circle, 4.5cm (1¾in) circle, small oval and small circle

Sugar glue

Small pair of scissors

Rolling pin

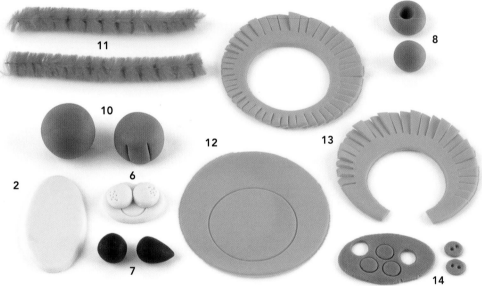

Instructions:

1 Make a brown body as shown on page 6, then make two holes in the front for the legs using the pointed tool.

2 Roll a small amount of of cream paste into a smooth ball, then flatten it into an thin oval for the tummy. Glue it in place with sugar glue then leave to dry.

3 Make the head as shown on page 6 using brown paste, then make two holes for the eyes with the pointed stick.

4 Insert stamens for the eyes. Using a fine black fibre-tip pen, mark the pupils with dots. Leave to dry.

5 Use the cream paste and small oval cutter to make a small flat oval shape for his muzzle and glue it on to the front of the face with sugar glue. Make a small hole at the top of the oval for the nose with the pointed tool.

6 Use a straw to make the mouth, then add two small balls of cream paste for the cheeks. Glue the cheeks in place with sugar glue, then use a cocktail stick or scriber to make little holes. Leave to dry.

7 Make a small cone of black paste and insert this into the nose hole using a small amount of sugar glue.

8 To make the ears, roll 2g (¹/₁₂oz) of brown paste into a smooth ball, then cut it in half and roll each piece into a ball again. Push the rounded end of a pointed tool into one ball but do not take the tool out. Add sugar glue to the bottom part of the ear and place it on the top of the head firmly. Remove the tool. Repeat with the other ear then leave to dry.

9 For the arms, roll 20g (²/₃oz) of brown paste into a smooth ball, cut it in half and roll each half into a sausage shape equal to the length of the body. Attach with a little sugar glue.

10 To make the paws and feet, roll 16g (½oz) of brown paste into a ball and cut it into four using the scissors. Shape each quarter into a flat oval disc. Mark each as shown with a cocktail stick and attach to the arms using sugar glue.

11 Cut an 8cm (3¼in) length of pipe cleaner. Apply glue to each end. Attach a foot to one end and push the other end into the body to make a leg. Repeat to make the other leg. Bend into shape when dry.

12 Roll out the tangerine paste with the rolling pin, but not too thinly. Make the mane by cutting out a circle using a 6cm (2⅜in) cutter. Next, cut out the middle, slightly off centre, using the 4.5cm (1¾in) circle cutter.

13 Snip with scissors all the way round to make a fringe, then cut the circle across the bottom edge. Glue the mane in place behind the ears. Repeat with a second circle of fringe, and support with foam if necessary.

14 Cut out small circles of blue paste for the buttons using the small circle cutter. Attach them with a little sugar glue, then mark them with a cocktail stick.

Chris

This little lion is the perfect candidate to decorate a child's birthday cake.

Frog

Materials:

100g (3½oz) lime green modelling paste

Small amounts of magenta, yellow and black modelling paste

Two green stripy pipe cleaners

Cocktail stick

Tools:

Basic tools (see page 7)

Small pair of scissors

Small thin palette knife

Sugar glue

Instructions:

1 Make a green body (see page 6) but do not make any holes in the front.

2 Roll 20g (⅔oz) of green paste into a smooth ball for the head, flatten it into an thin oval and mark it as shown using a cocktail stick.

3 Cut 4g (⅙oz) of green paste in half and roll each part into a smooth ball. With the round end of a pointed tool, make a large hole, insert a small ball of white paste then insert a small ball of black paste in the corner for the pupil. Repeat to make two eyes.

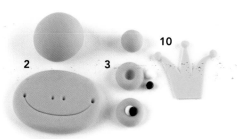

4 Cut 16g (½oz) of green paste into four. Shape each one into a flat oval disc and mark with a palette knife as shown to make the pads.

5 To make the ankles, cut 10g (⅓oz) of green paste into four and roll each one into a smooth round ball. With a little sugar glue, attach one on the top of each pad, then use a pointed tool to make a small hole on the top of each one.

6 For the arms, bend a 16cm (6¼in) green pipe cleaner in half, add a little sugar glue to the ends and attach a pad to each. Bend the pipe cleaner around the back of the cocktail stick, then glue it in place, bringing the pads down in front of the body.

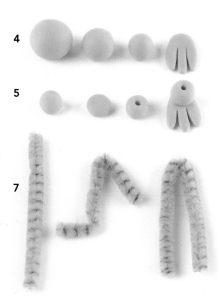

7 Cut two 11cm (4⅜in) lengths of pipe cleaner and shape as shown for the legs. Glue each end and attach a pad to one. Insert the other end into the base of the body at the back. Repeat with the other leg and pad.

8 Secure the head on to the cocktail stick using a little sugar glue while pressing down firmly. Attach the eyes on top of the head using a little sugar glue.

9 Roll out a small amount of yellow paste, shape it into a small crown and use sugar glue to attach it in place behind the eyes. Make three small balls of yellow paste for the top of the crown and glue them on.

10 Roll out the magenta paste and tie it into a bow, then use sugar glue to attach it at the top of the body.

Dave
The tiny frog is just a smaller version of
his dad, sitting in a watering can and
waiting to jump out.

Sheep

Materials:

100g (3½oz) white modelling paste

60g (2⅛oz) black modelling paste

Small amount of pink flower/gum paste

Two white stamens

One black pipe cleaner

Cocktail sticks

White wool

Tools:

Basic tools (see page 7)

Thin palette knife

Cutters: small oval, small circle

Small pair of scissors

Fine black fibre-tip pen

Sugar glue

Rolling pin

Instructions:

1 Make a white body as shown on page 6, insert a cocktail stick and make two holes in the front for the legs using the pointed tool.

2 For the fur, roll out the remaining 45g (1½oz) of white paste, not too thinly. Cut out small circles and roll each one into a ball, making them the same size. Starting at the base of the body glue them on individually in rows; continue going up the body until you reach the top. Try not to have any gaps between the balls.

3 Create the head by rolling 20g (⅔oz) of black sugarpaste into a ball and then into an oval. Make two holes for the nose.

4 Mark the mouth with the small circle cutter and use a pointed tool to make a small hole at each end.

5 For the eyes, roll 3g (⅛oz) of black paste into two balls. Using the pointed tool, make a hole in the middle, push in a stamen and mark it with a black pen. Attach the eyes to the top of the head with a little glue.

6 Cut a pipe cleaner in half and one piece in half again, making two 7.5cm (3in) legs and one 15cm (6in) arm length.

7 Make the hooves by rolling 16g (½oz) of black paste into a ball. Cut it in half and make two cones, then use a palette knife to mark a line down the front of each one. Add a little sugar glue to the ends of each 7.5cm (3in)pipe cleaner, attach one hoof to one end and insert the other end into the body at the front. Repeat for the other leg. Bend into shape when dry.

2 & 11

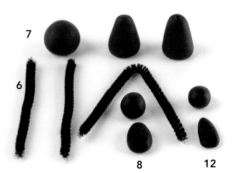

8 For the arms and hands, roll 5g (⅙oz) of black paste into a ball then cut it in half with scissors. Roll each half into a pear shape. Add sugar glue to each end of the 15cm (6in) pipe cleaner and attach the hands. Bend the pipe cleaner round the back of the cocktail stick and glue it in place, bringing the arms and hands in front.

9 Push the head on to the cocktail stick using a little sugar glue.

10 Use the small oval cutter to cut out two ears from black paste. Attach them to the top of the head with a little glue, supporting them with foam if necessary.

11 Following the instructions for step 2, make several small white balls and glue them on the top of the ears until the top of the head is covered. When dry, add roll out pink flower/gum paste and make a bow out of it. Secure this on top of the balls.

12 Roll a small piece of black paste into a cone, and glue it into place as a tail.

13 Make the knitting on cocktail sticks, using white wool, then attach it to the hands while the paste is still soft.

Beryl

A purple bow makes a great alternative.

Elephant

Materials:

110g (3⅞oz) grey modelling paste

Dark pink modelling paste

One grey pipe cleaner

Two white stamens

Miniature roses

Cocktail stick

Tools:

Basic tools (see page 7)

Thin palette knife

Small pair of scissors

Cutters: large heart,
  tiny heart

Fine black fibre-tip pen

Sugar glue

Instructions:

1 Make a grey body, as shown on page 6, then make two holes in the front for the legs with the pointed tool.

2 Make the head by rolling 20g (⅔oz) of grey paste into a ball, and shaping as shown. Use a pointed tool to make a hole in the end of the trunk and two holes for the eyes. Support the head on a cocktail stick. Turn the trunk up over the head, supporting it if necessary, and use the smiley tool to make a small mouth under the trunk. Insert stamens for the eyes, using a black pen to mark the dots. Leave to dry.

3 Roll out a small amount of grey paste and cut out two large hearts for the ears. Leave to dry.

4 Roll 20g (⅔oz) of grey paste into a ball and cut it into four pieces with the scissors. Roll each piece into a ball and then press it into a flat disc. Use the palette knife to mark each as shown to make the feet. Place one on each side of the body.

5 Make the arms by rolling 20g (⅔oz) of grey paste into a smooth ball and cutting it in half with scissors, then rolling each half into a sausage shape the length of the body from the shoulder to the top of the foot. Glue each in place.

6 To make the legs, cut two 7cm (2¾in) lengths of pipe cleaner. Add sugar glue to each end, attach a foot to one end and insert the other end into the body. Repeat with the other leg and foot.

7 Attach the head to the body with a little glue, then attach the ears. Flatten a small ball of grey sugarpaste and attach it to the body as a tail.

8 Roll out a small amount of dark pink sugarpaste and cut out tiny pink hearts. Glue these to the feet and tummy. Make a bow from the sugarpaste and attach it below the head using sugar glue.

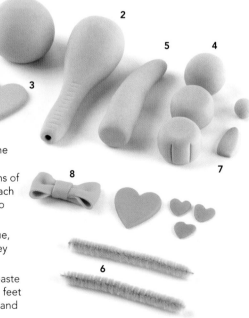

Zebra

Materials:

80g (2⅔oz) white modelling paste

50g (1⅔oz) black modelling paste

Small amount of royal blue modelling paste

One black pipe cleaner

Two white stamens

Cocktail stick

Tools:

Basic tools (see page 7)

Thin palette knife

Small pair of scissors

Cutters: tiny blossom, circle

Fine black fibre-tip pen

Sugar glue

Rolling pin

Instructions:

1 Make a white body as shown on page 6 and insert an 8cm (3¼in) cocktail stick. Make two holes in the front for the legs using the pointed tool.

2 Create a head by rolling 20g (⅔oz) of white paste into a ball and then into a pear shape. Make two holes for the eyes with the pointed tool. Insert stamens into the holes, then use a black pen to mark the pupils.

3 Roll out a small circle of black paste to fit over the end of the nose and use sugar glue to attach it in place as the muzzle. Make two small holes for the nostrils with the pointed tool. Mark the mouth with a circle cutter then use the pointed tool to make a hole at each end.

4 Make the hooves by rolling 25g (⅞oz) of black paste into a ball, cutting it into four and shaping each part into a cone. Use a palette knife to mark a line down the front of each one.

5 Cut a pipe cleaner in half and one piece in half again. You now have two 7.5cm (3in) legs and one 15cm (6in) arm length. Add sugar glue to each end of a 7.5cm (3in) length, attach a hoof to one end and insert the other end into the body at the front. Repeat for the second leg and bend each into shape when dry.

6 Add sugar glue to each end of the 15cm (6in) pipe cleaner and attach a hoof to each end. Bend the pipe cleaner round the back of the cocktail stick and glue it in place before bringing the arms and hooves to the front.

7 Push the head on to the cocktail stick, securing it using a little sugar glue.

8 To make the ears, roll 2g (1/12oz) of white paste into a ball. Cut the ball in half, roll each piece into a ball again and push the rounded end of a pointed tool into one ball. Do not take the tool out, but glue the bottom part of the ear and place it on the top of the head firmly. Pinch the top of the paste to make a pointed ear, then remove the tool. Repeat with the other ear and leave to dry.

9 Create a mane by rolling out a strip of black paste. Snip it with scissors as shown and roll it up before lightly gluing it in place between the ears for a fluffy mane.

10 When the zebra is completely dry, mark the stripes as shown using a black pen.

11 Use the blossom cutter to make some small blue blossoms and decorate the zebra. Secure them in place with stamens.

Lynne

This chic little zebra would make a characterful topper for any white cake.

Chick

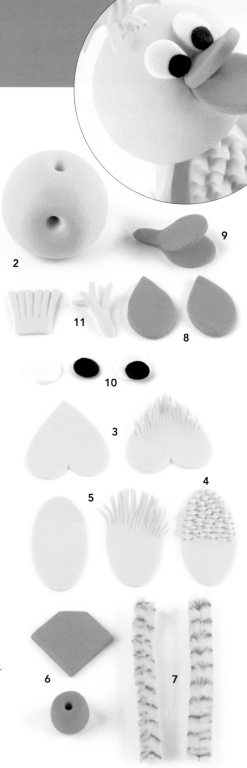

Materials:

100g (3½oz) yellow modelling paste

Small amounts of orange, white and black modelling paste

One yellow or orange pipe cleaner

Cocktail stick

Tools:

Basic tools (see page 7)

Cutters: various size oval, small round, small square, very small petal, heart

Thin palette knife

Small pair of scissors

Sugar glue

Rolling pin

Instructions:

1 Make a yellow body as shown on page 6, insert an 8cm (3¼in) cocktail stick, then make two holes in the front for the legs with the pointed tool.

2 Roll 20g (¾oz) of yellow paste into a ball for the head and shape as shown. Using a pointed tool, make a hole in the middle of the face for the beak and one at the top of the head for the feathers. Attach the head to the body with a little glue.

3 Roll out the yellow paste and use the heart cutter to cut one heart shape as the basis for the tail. Snip the top with scissors as shown, then use sugar glue to attach it to the back of the body with the round ends tucked under the base. Fluff out the tail to look like feathers.

4 Using yellow paste and the oval cutter, cut out one large oval for the tummy. Use the scissors to cut into the paste as shown, then lightly glue it and attach to the front of the body.

5 Cut out another two large ovals of yellow paste for the wings. Snip the narrow end of one and attach the other end of it to the back of the body with sugar glue before bringing it forward as shown. Repeat to make the second wing.

6 Use the small square cutter to cut out two small squares from the orange paste to form the basis for the feet. Cut off one small corner from each with scissors. Roll 5g (⅙oz) of orange paste into a ball then cut it in two. Roll each half into a ball and place one on top of each foot using a little sugar glue.

7 Cut two 7cm (2¾in) lengths of pipe cleaner, and add sugar glue to each end. Attach a foot to one end and insert the other end into the body. Repeat with the other leg and foot.

8 Make the parts for a beak by rolling out the orange pages and cutting out two small petal shapes with the petal cutter.

9 Join the parts of the beak together with a little glue at the pointed end and push them into the hole at the front of the head using the pointed tool.

10 For the eyes, use cutters to cut out two small ovals of white paste and two very small circles of black paste. Using a little glue attach the white ovals on the face just above the beak, then glue the black circles on top, as shown.

11 Roll out a small thin strip of yellow paste, snip with scissors and roll up as shown. With a pointed tool, push the feathers into the top of the head using a little glue.

Kaz
The baby chick on the right is made in the same way as Kaz, only half the size. The eyes are two small black dots added using a black fibre-tip pen.

Sunflower Fairy

Materials:

60g (2⅛oz) dark green
  modelling paste

50g (1⅔oz) brown modelling
  paste or chocolate paste

Small amount of yellow flower/
  gum paste

Yellow and green striped
  pipe cleaner

Two white stamens

Cocktail sticks

Tools:

Basic tools (see
  page 7)

Cutters: large daisy,
  tiny blossom

Thin palette knife

Small pair of scissors

Fine black fibre-tip pen

Sugar glue

Instructions:

1 Make a green body as shown
on page 6, insert an 8cm (3¼in)
cocktail stick and make two
holes in the front for the legs
with the pointed tool.

2 For the head, roll a 20g
(⅔oz) ball of brown paste into
a smooth ball. Support it on a
cocktail stick and use a pointed
tool to make the holes for the
eyes and nose, and the smiley
tool for the mouth. Insert
two stamens for the eyes
and mark the pupils with
a fine black fibre-tip pen.

3 Make a nose by rolling a
small ball of brown paste into
a round-ended cone, then insert
it into the hole and secure using
a little glue.

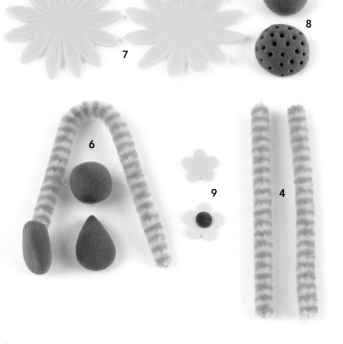

4 Cut a pipe cleaner in half and one piece in half again. You now have two
legs of 7.5cm (3in) and one arm length of 15cm (6in).

5 For the shoes, roll 12g (⁵⁄₁₂oz) of green paste into a ball then use the
scissors to cut it in half to make two flat ovals. Lightly glue both ends of one
7.5cm (3in) length of pipe cleaner, then insert one end into the shoe and the
other end into the body. Repeat for the other leg. Bend each pipe cleaner
into shape when dry.

6 To make the hands, roll 3g (⅛oz) of brown paste into a ball. Cut the ball in half to make two ovals. Add a little sugar glue to each end of the 15cm (6in) pipe cleaner and attach the hands. Bend the pipe cleaner around the back of the cocktail stick and glue in place, bringing the arms and hands down.

7 Roll out the yellow paste and use the daisy cutter to cut out five flowers. Soften the petal edges with the rounded end of a pointed tool, then, using a little sugar glue, place a flower on top of the pipe cleaner. Repeat with a second flower. Glue the head on firmly and attach three more flowers to the top of the head as shown.

8 Roll a small ball of brown paste into a flat disc and glue it on top of the flowers on the top of the head. Make little holes in the paste with a cocktail stick.

9 Decorate the feet with two tiny blossoms cut from yellow paste with tiny dots of brown paste glued in the centre.

Louise
This sunny character would make an ideal Easter cake topper, or she might make a fun decoration for your window sill.

Dinosaur

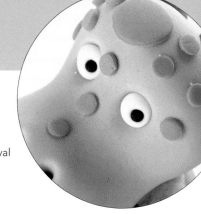

Materials:

120g (4¼oz) pale blue
  modelling paste

Small amount of orange
  flower/gum paste

Small amount of white paste

Two black stamens or two very
  small balls of black paste

One pale blue pipe cleaner

Cocktail stick

Tools:

Basic tools (see page 7)

Thin palette knife

Cutters: large circle, small oval

Small circle cutter or
  icing nozzles

Small pair of scissors

Sugar glue

Instructions:

1 Make a pale blue body as
shown on page 6; make two
holes at the front for the legs.

2 For the head, roll 23g (⅞oz)
of pale blue paste into
a ball and then shape
as shown. Use the
pointed tool to make
two holes for the eyes
and two holes for
the nostrils, then use
a large circle cutter to
shape the mouth and make
a small hole at each end
with a pointed tool.

3 To make the eyes, shape
two very small balls of white
paste into tear drops and
insert into the holes
using a little sugar
glue. Next, push in
a black stamen or
use very small balls of
black paste.

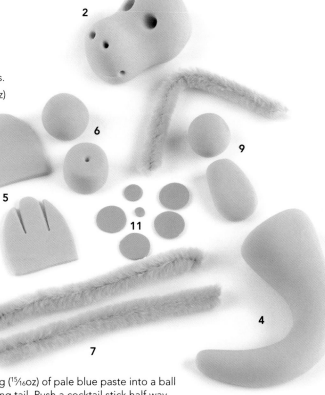

4 Make the tail by rolling 24g (¹⁵⁄₁₆oz) of pale blue paste into a ball
and rolling one end into a long tail. Push a cocktail stick half way
into the back of the body at the base for extra support and push on
the tail, using a little glue to secure it. Leave to dry.

5 Roll out two pale blue ovals for the feet and cut a small piece
away from one end. Use the palette knife to make two cuts through
the paste for the toes.

6 To make the ankles, roll two small balls of pale blue paste, flatten them slightly and glue them on to the feet.

7 Cut two 9cm (3½in) lengths of pipe cleaner for the legs and one 10cm (4in) length for the arms.

8 Lightly glue each end of a 9cm (3½in) pipe cleaner and insert one end into the foot and ankle and the other end into the body. Repeat for the second leg.

9 Roll 5g (⅙oz) of paste into a ball and cut it in half with the scissors to make two oval hands. Add a little sugar glue to each end of the 10cm (4in) pipe cleaner and attach the hands. Bend the pipe cleaner around the back of the cocktail stick, then glue it in place, bringing the arms and hands down.

10 Push the head on to the cocktail stick firmly using a little sugar glue. Leave to dry.

11 Cut out different size circles of orange paste for the spots, and attach them to the dinosaur with a little glue.

Charlie

Whatever colours you use for this cute little dinosaur's skin and dots, he will still look very fierce.

Bee

Materials:

60g (2⅛oz) yellow modelling paste

60g (2⅛oz) black modelling paste

Two black pipe cleaners

Two white stamens

Butterfly wings

Yellow glitter

Cocktail stick

Novelty bucket

Tools:

Basic tools (see page 7)

Fine black fibre-tip pen

Small pair of scissors

Cutters: small heart, tiny blossom

Sugar glue

Rolling pin

Instructions:

1 Make a yellow body as shown on page 6, then make two holes at the front for the legs with the pointed tool.

2 Roll out the black paste and cut four thin strips. Wrap them around the body as shown, then glue them in place with sugar glue. Cut out three tiny blossoms from yellow paste using the blossom cutter and attach them to the middle of the top three black strips with a little glue.

3 Roll 20g (⅔oz) of black paste into a ball for the head.

4 Cut out a heart shape from white paste and glue it on to the front of the face. Use the pointed tool to make two holes for the eyes, two small holes at the top of the head for the antennae, a hole for the nose and then use a smiley tool to shape the mouth.

5 Make a nose using a small cone of black paste and insert it into the nose hole using a small amount of sugar glue. Insert stamens for the eyes, and use a black fibre-tip pen to mark the pupils.

6 For the antennae, roll 3g (⅛oz) of yellow paste into a ball, then cut it in half and make two smaller balls.

7 Cut a black pipe cleaner into two 4cm (1½in) lengths, glue one end and attach a yellow ball. Lightly glue the ball and dip it into the glitter. Shake off the excess, glue the other end and push into the head. Repeat for the other antenna.

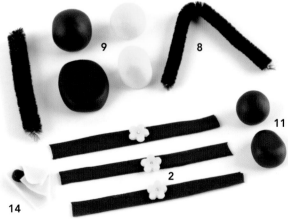

8 Cut two 7cm (2¾in) lengths of pipe cleaner for the legs and one 11cm (4¼in) length for the arms.

9 To make the shoes, roll 10g (⅓oz) of black paste into a ball and cut in half to make two flat ovals. Make the socks with a 6g ball (¼oz) of yellow paste: cut the ball in half with scissors and roll each piece into a small ball, then attach one on top of each shoe with a little glue.

10 Lightly glue each end of a 7cm (2¾in) pipe cleaner and insert one end into the sock and shoe and the other end into the body. Repeat for the other leg.

11 For the hands, roll 5g (⅙oz) of paste into a ball, then cut it in half to make two ovals. Add a little sugar glue to each end of the 11cm (4¼in)

pipe cleaner and attach the hands. Bend the pipe cleaner around the back of the cocktail stick and glue in place, bringing the arms and hands down.

12 Push the head on to the cocktail stick in the body, using a little sugar glue to secure it.

13 Decorate the bee with butterfly wings and tiny blossoms, made with white sugarpaste and the blossom cutter, securing them with gold or orange stamens in the centres.

14 To make the baby bees in the bucket, make a very tiny sausage shape with black paste, then roll out a small square of pink or blue paste and wrap the baby bee in the blanket.

Carol
This industrious bee is carrying her children to work in her pollen bucket. If you can not find ready-made wings, you can make them from sugarpaste, paper or any other material.

Piggy

Materials:

100g (3½oz) peach coloured modelling paste

Small amounts of jade and white modelling paste

Two orange pipe cleaners

Two white stamens

Green stamens or sugar beads

Cocktail stick

Tools:

Basic tools (see page 7)

Thin palette knife

Cutters: small heart, tiny blossom, alphabet letter

Small pair of scissors

Fine black fibre-tip pen

Sugar paste

Instructions:

1 Make a peach coloured body as shown on page 6. Insert a cocktail stick and use the pointed tool to make two holes in the front for the legs.

2 Roll 20g (⅔oz) of peach coloured paste into a smooth ball for the head. Make two holes for the eyes with the pointed tool.

3 For the snout, roll 5g (⅙oz) of peach coloured paste into a smooth ball and flatten it slightly. Using a little glue, attach it to the front of the head. Insert the pointed tool and make two holes for the snout.

4 Roll 20g (⅔oz) of peach coloured paste into a ball and cut it into four pieces for the feet. Roll each piece into a ball and then press it gently into the form of a flattened disc. Mark it as shown.

5 For the legs, cut two 7cm (2¾in) lengths of pipe cleaner and add glue to each end. Attach a foot to one end and insert the other end into the body, then repeat with the other leg and foot.

6 Bend a 14cm (5½in) orange pipe cleaner in half for the arms. Add a little sugar glue to each end and attach a foot. Bend the pipe cleaner around the back of the cocktail stick, then glue it in place, bringing the feet down beside the body.

7 Push the head on to the cocktail stick using a little sugar glue. Press down firmly.

8 Roll 2g (¹⁄₁₂oz) of peach coloured paste into a smooth ball, then cut it in half and roll each piece into a ball again. Push the rounded end of a pointed tool into one ball. Without taking the tool out, glue the bottom part of the ear and place it on the top of the head firmly. Pinch the top of the paste to make a pointed ear then remove the tool. Repeat for the second ear.

9 Twist 10cm (4in) of pipe cleaner around the pointed tool, then glue and push one end into the base of the body at the back for a curly tail.

10 Cut out a heart from jade paste using the heart cutter and attach it to the tummy with sugar glue.

11 Using the cutters, cut out one letter and five tiny blossoms from white paste. Glue the letter on top of the heart and secure the blossoms in place with green stamens.

Alan

The letter on the piggy's tummy can be changed to the initial of the recipient.

Flower Fairy

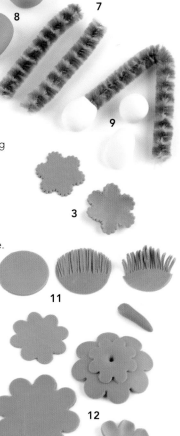

Materials:

60g (2⅛oz) red modelling paste

25g (⅚oz) flesh coloured modelling paste

10g (⅓oz) dark green flower/gum paste

Small amount of white and brown flower/gum paste

Green stripy pipe cleaner

Butterfly wings

Small yellow stamens or sugar balls

Cocktail stick

Tools:

Basic tools (see page 7)

Cutters: small circle, large blossom or carnation, medium blossom, tiny blossom

Fine black fibre-tip pen

Small scissors

Sugar glue

Rolling pin

Instructions:

1 Make a red body as shown on page 6, insert an 8cm (3¼in) cocktail stick and make two holes in the front for the legs with the pointed tool.

2 Use the blossom cutter to cut out tiny blossoms from white sugar paste and decorate the body, securing them in place with a little sugar glue. Add yellow stamens.

3 Roll out the green paste and cut out two circles using a carnation cutter. Frill the edges to complete the leg frills. Using a little sugar glue, place one over each leg hole, then push a pointed tool though to remake the holes.

4 Roll a 20g (⅔oz) ball of flesh coloured paste into a smooth ball for the head. Use a pointed tool to make a hole for the nose and use the smiley tool to mark the mouth.

5 Roll a small ball of flesh-coloured paste into a cone for the nose. Insert it into the hole using a small amount of sugar glue.

6 When the head is completely dry, draw the eyes on using a fine black pen, or follow the instructions for the Sunflower Fairy (see page 20).

7 Cut a pipe cleaner in half and one piece in half again. You now have two 7.5cm (3in) legs and one 15cm (6in) arm length.

8 For the shoes, roll 12g (⁵⁄₁₂oz) of red paste into a ball then cut it in half with scissors to make two ovals. Lightly glue both ends of the pipe cleaner, then insert one end into the shoe and the other end into the body. Repeat for the other leg.

9 To make the hands, roll 5g (⅙oz) of flesh coloured paste into a ball, then cut it in half to make two ovals. Add a little sugar glue to each end of the 15cm (6in) pipe cleaner and attach the hands. Bend the pipe cleaner around the back of the cocktail stick and glue it in place, bringing the arms and hands down. Push the head on to the cocktail stick using a little glue.

10 Roll out the green paste and make two blossoms with the medium cutter. Soften the petal edges with the rounded end of the pointed tool, add glue to the cocktail stick and place the frills on individually, pressing them down firmly at the front and back.

11 Roll out brown paste and cut two circles with the small circle cutter. Take each circle and snip the edge half way round before carefully fluffing the strands out. Glue each one individually on to the head as hair. Work all the way round to cover the head with two rows. The hole in the middle will be covered by the hat.

12 For the hat, cut out one large and one medium blossom in green paste. Soften the edges with the rounded end of the pointed tool, then glue it on top of the hair. With the pointed tool, make a hole in the middle and insert a small green stalk.

13 Use sugar glue to attach a pair of butterfly wings to finish.

Jane

This little delightful fairy can be made in any colour. Make sure you glue her down on the cake so she does not fly away!

Bear

Materials:

110g (3¾oz) cream modelling or chocolate paste

Small amount of light brown and black paste

Ribbon bow

Two white stamens

One brown pipe cleaner

Cocktail stick

Tools:

Basic tools (see page 7)

Cutters: small oval, small circle

Fine black fibre-tip pen

Confectioner's varnish

Rolling pin

Palette knife

Small scissors

Sugar glue

Instructions:

1 Make a cream body as shown as page 6, insert an 8cm (3¼in) cocktail stick and make two holes for the legs in the front with the pointed tool. Roll out a small amount of light brown paste and use the oval cutter to cut out an oval for the tummy. Use sugar glue to secure it in place.

2 Roll 20g (⅔oz) of cream paste into a ball for the head, then use a pointed tool to make two holes for the eyes. Insert stamens into the holes, then use a fine black fibre-tip pen to mark the pupils.

3 Roll a small ball of light brown paste, then gently press it with the rolling pin to make a small flat oval shape for a muzzle. Glue it on to the front of the face. Make a small hole at the top of the oval for the nose. Use a palette knife to mark the mouth.

4 Make a small cone of black paste and insert it into the nose hole using a small amount of sugar glue. Next, use a cocktail stick to make a few small holes around the mouth.

5 For the ears, roll 2g (¹⁄₁₂oz) of cream paste into a ball. Cut it in half and roll each piece into a ball again. Push the rounded end of a pointed tool into one ball. Glue the bottom part of the ear and place it firmly on the top of the head. Remove the tool and repeat with the other ear. Leave to dry.

6 Make two arms by rolling 20g (⅔oz) of cream paste into a smooth ball, cutting it in half and rolling each half into a sausage shape equal to the length of the body. Attach both arms to the body with a little glue.

7 To make the paws, roll 16g (½oz) of cream paste into a ball. Cut it into four with scissors and shape each quarter into an oval disc. Attach one to the front of each arm.

8 Cut two 7cm (2¾in) lengths of pipe cleaner for the legs. Add glue to each end, then attach a paw to one end and insert the other end into the body. Repeat with the other leg and paw.

9 Using the light brown paste with the circle cutters, cut out two small and six very small circles and lightly glue them on to the front of the paws as shown with sugar glue.

10 For the tail, fold 5cm (2in) of pipe cleaner in half and twist the ends together. Use a little glue to insert it in the base at the back.

11 Decorate the bear with a ribbon bow and varnish the nose with confectioner's varnish.

Maggie
The baby bear uses smaller amounts of paste, but is otherwise made the same way as his mummy.

Mouse

Materials:

100g (3½oz) pink modelling paste

Small amounts of white and dark pink paste

Pink pipe cleaner

Pastry brush for whiskers

Two white stamens

Cocktail sticks

Miniature flowers

Tools:

Basic tools (see page 7)

Palette knife

Cutters: large circle, small circle, small oval

Small pair of scissors

Fine black fibre-tip pen

Sugar glue

Rolling pin

Instructions:

1 Make a pink body as shown on page 6 and insert an 8cm (3¼in) cocktail stick. Make two holes in the front for the legs.

2 Using a small amount of white paste, cut out an oval for the tummy, and glue in place.

3 Roll 20g (⅔oz) of pink paste into a smooth ball, then shape as shown for the head. Use a pointed tool to make holes for the eyes and nose. Insert two stamens for the eyes and mark the pupils using a black pen.

4 Roll a medium size ball of dark pink paste into a cone for the nose. Using a little glue, insert into the hole.

5 Use the scissors to cut a few bristles from the pastry brush and push them into the cheeks on each side of the face for the whiskers.

6 Mark the mouth with a circle cutter and use a pointed tool to make a hole at each end.

7 Use the circle cutters to cut out two pink outer ears and two white smaller inner ears. Do not roll the paste too thinly. Glue half a cocktail stick between the outer and inner ear and press down around the edges only. Push the assembled ears through the top of the head and leave to dry.

8 Cut a pipe cleaner in half and one piece in half again to make two 7.5cm (3in) legs and one 15cm (6in) arm length.

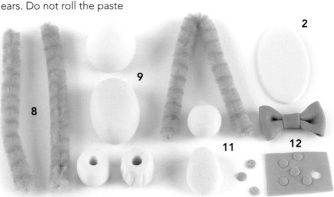

9 To make the shoes, roll 16g (½oz) of pink paste into a ball and cut it in half to make two flat ovals. Use 10g (⅓oz) of paste to make the socks by rolling it into two small balls, making a hole in the top of each and then marking around the edges with a cocktail stick as shown. Secure one sock on top of each shoe with a little sugar glue.

10 Lightly glue one end of a 7.5cm (3in) pipe cleaner and insert into a sock and shoe. Lightly glue the other end of the pipe cleaner and insert into the body. Shape when dry. Repeat for the other leg.

11 For the hands, roll 6g (¼oz) of pink paste into a ball then cut it in half to make two ovals. Add sugar glue to each end of the 15cm (6in) pipe cleaner and attach the hands. Bend the pipe cleaner around the back of the cocktail stick, glue it in place and bring the arms and hands down. Bend the arms into shape once the glue is dry.

12 Push the head on to the cocktail stick using a little sugar glue, then decorate with buttons and bows made from dark pink paste. Add a bunch of miniature flowers for a cute mouse.

Anglia

A sugar mouse can hide from his beloved in a teacup if you make him slightly smaller!

Dog

Materials:

110g (3¾oz) light brown modelling paste

Small amounts of royal blue, pink, red and black modelling paste

One beige pipe cleaner

Two white stamens

Blue sugar bow or ribbon

Brown dusting powder

Tools:

Basic tools (see page 7)

Cutters: large oval, small oval, small round

Fine black fibre-tip pen

Confectioner's varnish

Palette knife

Sugar glue

Rolling pin

Small pair of scissors

Instructions:

1 Make a light brown body as shown on page 6 and insert an 8cm (3¼in) cocktail stick. Do not make any holes for the legs.

2 Roll out a small amount of pink paste and use the large oval cutter to make an oval for the tummy. Secure it in place with sugar glue.

3 For the head, roll 20g (⅔oz) of light brown paste into a ball and shape as shown. Support it on a cocktail stick and make a small hole in the middle of the face for the nose and two for the eyes.

4 Insert a white stamen into each eye and use a fine black fibre-tip pen to mark the pupils. Using a palette knife, mark a small line across to mark the mouth and make a line down from the nose. Use a pointed tool to insert a very small ball of red paste for the tongue and secure it with sugar glue.

5 Make a nose from a small cone of black paste and insert it into the hole in the head with a small amount of sugar glue.

6 Roll out a small amount of pink paste and use the small oval cutter to make two small ovals as ears. Place them on the top of the head. Support if necessary and leave to dry.

7 Roll 12g (⁵⁄₁₂oz) of light brown paste into a ball, cut it in half with scissors and roll out one half again into a sausage shape. Using a little glue, attach the leg around the base of the body and mark as shown with the palette knife. Repeat with the other leg and leave both to dry.

8 For the paws, roll 12g (⁵⁄₁₂oz) of light brown paste into a smooth ball and cut it in half. Roll each half into a smooth ball and mark with a palette knife as shown.

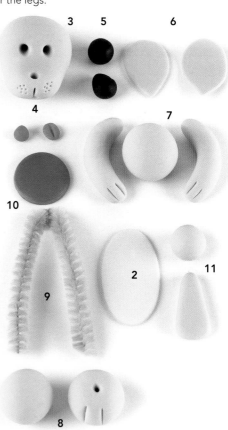

9 Cut a 15cm (6in) length of beige pipe cleaner to form the arms. Glue and attach a paw to each end, then bend it round the back of the cocktail stick. Glue the arms in place and bring the arms and paws to the front.

10 For the collar, roll out a circle of blue paste (not too thinly). Using a little glue, place it over the middle of the cocktail stick and gently press down. Take the head from its support and press it firmly over the collar.

11 Make a small oval of light brown paste with the small oval cutter and attach it to the back of the body with a little glue, to form the tail.

12 Roll out royal blue sugarpaste and make a bow. Secure it on the top of the head with sugar glue.

13 To make the patches, use a brush to dust small circles of powder on the dog. For a shiny nose, paint it with confectioner's varnish and leave to dry.

Rob
This faithful chap will be happy to guard your sweet treats!

Bunny

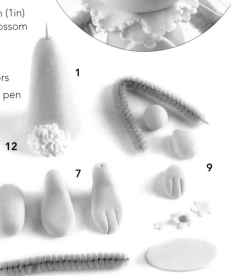

Materials:

100g (3½oz) light brown modelling paste

Small amount of pink flower/gum paste

20g (⅔oz) of white sugarpaste

Two light brown pipe cleaners

Two white stamens

Cocktail stick

Pastry brush

Tools:

Basic tools (see page 7)

Cutters: large oval, small oval, 2.5cm (1in) blossom, tiny blossom

Sieve or clay gun

Thin palette knife

Small pair of scissors

Fine black fibre-tip pen

Rolling pin

Pin

Sugar glue

Instructions:

1 Make a light brown body as shown on page 6. Insert an 8cm (3¼in) cocktail stick and make two holes in the front for the legs. Using a small amount of pink paste with the small oval cutter, cut out an oval for the tummy and glue it in place.

2 Roll 20g (⅔oz) of light brown paste into a smooth ball for the head and attach it to a cocktail stick. Use the pointed tool to make a small hole in the middle of the face for the nose and a small hole for the mouth, then use a thin palette knife to cut a line from the nose to the mouth.

3 Make a small cone of pink paste for the nose and insert it into the hole with a little sugar glue.

4 For the mouth, roll a very small ball of pink paste and push it into the face using the pointed tool.

5 Cut a few bristles from a pastry brush and push them into the cheeks on both sides of the mouth as whiskers. Trim if necessary, then use a pin to make a few small dots around the whiskers.

6 Without rolling the paste too thinly, cut out two light brown outer ears and two smaller pink inner ears using the oval cutters. Glue half a cocktail stick in place between one of the outer and inner ears and press down around the edges only. Next, push it into the top of the head. Repeat with the second ear and leave to dry.

7 Roll 15g (½oz) of light brown paste into a ball, then cut it in half to make two large oval feet. Cut two slits for the toes, and gently curve them over a pointed tool. Smooth and shape the feet as shown.

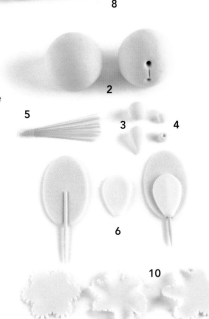

8 Cut two 10cm (4in) lengths of pipe cleaner for legs. Glue each end, attach a foot to one end and push the other end into the body. Repeat.

9 Roll 5g (⅙oz) of light brown paste into a ball, cut it in half and shape each half into a tear drop. Cut two small slits at the end of these paws and curl the ends over a pointed tool. Add a little sugar glue to both ends of a 14cm (5¾in) length of pipe cleaner and attach the paws. Bend the pipe cleaner around the back of the cocktail stick, then glue it in place and bring the arms and paws down.

10 For the neck frills, cut out two circles of pink paste using a 2.5cm (1in) blossom cutter. Frill the edges, add glue to the cocktail stick and the top of the pipe cleaner and place the frills over the cocktail stick.

11 Push the head on to the cocktail stick using a little sugar glue and press down firmly. Using a black pen, draw two small round dots just above the nose for the eyes and leave to dry.

12 Push 20g (⅔oz) of white sugarpaste through a clay gun or sieve to make a fluffy tail. Attach it to the base of the body using a little glue. Decorate between the ears in the same way as the tail, making a fluffy mop. Finally, make some pink blossoms with the tiny blossom cutter to decorate the rabbit, gluing them on to the wrists and feet with sugar glue.

Amelia

If you do not want me to have long legs cut the pipe cleaners shorter, but I like my feet big.

Ladybird

Materials:

50g (1⅔oz) red modelling paste

60g (2⅛oz) black modelling paste

Small amount of white modelling paste

One red stripy pipe cleaner

One black pipe cleaner

Two white stamens

Red glitter

Butterfly wings

Cocktail stick

Tools:

Basic tools (see page 7)

Thin palette knife

Cocktail stick

Small circle cutters

Large icing tube

Small pair of scissors

Fine black fibre-tip pen

Sugar glue

Instructions:

1 Make a red body as shown on page 6. Insert an 8cm (3¼in) cocktail stick and make two holes in the front for the legs.

2 Roll a 20g (⅔oz) ball of black paste into a smooth ball for the head. Cut out a small white circle of modelling paste and glue it on to the front. Use a pointed tool to make two small holes for the eyes, one in the middle of the face for the nose, a small hole below that for the mouth and two holes on the top of the head for the antennae.

3 Roll 3g (⅛oz) of red paste into a ball, cut in half and make two smaller balls. Cut the black pipe cleaner into two 5cm (2in) lengths, add glue to one end and attach a red ball. Lightly cover the ball with glue and dip it into the glitter. Shake off the excess. Push the other end into the top of the head with a little glue. Repeat for the second antenna.

4 Cut out thirty circles from black sugarpaste using the small circle cutters. Use a little glue to attach them on to the body.

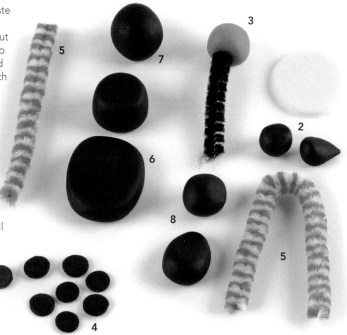

5 Cut a pipe cleaner in half and one piece in half again, to make two 7.5cm (3in) legs and one 15cm (6in) arm length.

6 Roll 10g of black paste into a ball and cut it in half with the scissors to make two flat ovals for the shoes.

7 Make socks by rolling 6g (¼oz) of black paste into two small balls and placing one on top of each shoe with a little glue. Lightly glue each end of a 7.5cm (3in) pipe cleaner and insert one end into the sock and shoe, and the other end into the body. Repeat.

8 For the hands, roll 6g (¼oz) of black paste into a ball before cutting it in half to make two balls. Add glue to each end of the 15cm (6in) pipe cleaner and attach one hand to each end. Bend the pipe cleaner around the back of the cocktail stick and glue it in place, bringing the arms and hands down. Bend the arms into shape when dry.

9 Attach the head to the body with a little sugar glue. Place the butterfly wings at the back and secure with glue or royal icing.

Judith

This wobbly ladybird is struggling to count how many dots she has. Can you help her out?

Wobbly Dolly

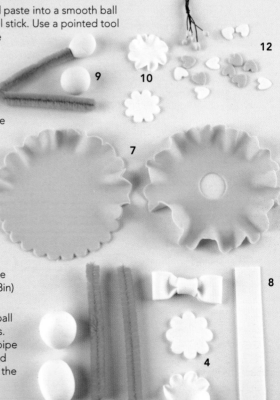

Materials:

80g (2⅔oz) blue modelling paste

40g (1⅓oz) flesh coloured
   modelling paste

Small amount of white modelling paste

One blue pipe cleaner

Two white stamens

Pale blue stamens or sugar balls

Pale yellow royal icing

Cocktail sticks

Tools:

Basic tools (see
page 7)

Thin palette knife

Small pair of scissors

Fine black fibre-tip pen

Cutters: tiny heart, blossom or
carnation, small blossom, Garrett frill

No. 2 icing nozzle and piping bag

Sugar glue

Instructions:

1 Make a blue body as shown on page 6 and insert an 8cm (3¼in)
cocktail stick into it. Make two holes in the front for the legs using
the pointed tool.

2 Roll a 20g (⅔oz) ball of flesh coloured paste into a smooth ball
for the head and support it on a cocktail stick. Use a pointed tool
to make a hole for the nose and use the
smiley tool to mark the mouth.

3 Roll a small ball of paste into a cone
for the nose. Using a little glue, insert
into the hole in the head. When the
head is completely dry, draw on the
eyes using a fine black pen, or follow the
instructions for the Sunflower Fairy (see
page 20).

4 Make two leg frills by rolling out
white paste and cutting out two
circles using a blossom or carnation
cutter. Frill the edges of both pieces
with the rounded end of the pointed
tool, then use a little sugar glue to
secure them over the leg holes. Use a
pointed tool to remake the holes.

5 Cut a pipe cleaner in half then cut one
piece in half again to make two 7.5cm (3in)
legs and one 15cm (6in) arm length.

6 Roll 12g (⁵⁄₁₂oz) of white paste into a ball
and cut it in half to make two oval shoes.
Lightly glue both ends of a 7.5cm (3in) pipe
cleaner, insert one end into the shoe and
the other end into the body. Repeat for the
second leg.

40

7 Cut out a circle of blue paste using a Garrett frill cutter to make the skirt. Frill the outer edge with the rounded end of the pointed tool, then use the large end of the no. 2 icing nozzle to cut out a hole in the middle. Add glue to the body just above the leg frills. Pull the skirt down over the cocktail stick, supporting it with foam if necessary.

8 Roll out a thin strip of white paste and glue it around the top of the skirt. Use scissors to trim it to fit, then attach a bow at the back.

9 Roll 5g (⅙oz) of flesh coloured paste into a ball, and cut in half to make two oval hands. Add a little sugar glue to each end of the 15cm (6in) pipe cleaner and attach the hands. Bend the pipe cleaner around the back of the cocktail stick and glue it in place, bringing the arms and hands down. Shape into position when dry.

10 Roll out some white paste and cut two medium size blossoms for neck frills. Soften the edges with the rounded end of the pointed tool, add glue to the cocktail stick and place the frills on individually. Press down firmly at the front and back over the pipe cleaner before gluing the head on firmly.

11 With a small amount of pale yellow royal icing, pipe small circles all over the head as hair, then add blue blossoms, securing them in place by adding blue stamens to the centre.

12 Cut out hearts from blue and white sugarpaste with the tiny heart cutter and use them to decorate the dress and shoes, securing them with sugar glue.

Doreen

This wobbly dolly would make a fun topper for a little girl's birthday cake – but don't feel you have to let the little ones have all the fun!

Cow

Materials:

100g (3½oz) brown modelling paste

20g (⅔oz) dark brown modelling paste

Small amounts of white and pink modelling paste

Two brown pipe cleaners

Four pink stamens or sugar balls and two white stamens

Small bell and pink ribbon

Cocktail stick

Tools:

Basic tools (see page 7)

Cutter: oval

Sieve or clay gun

Thin palette knife

Small pair of scissors

Fine black fibre-tip pen

Sugar glue

Instructions:

1 Make a brown body as shown on page 6 and insert an 8cm (3¼in) cocktail stick. Make two holes in the front for the legs with the pointed tool. Roll out pink paste, cut out a small oval with the small oval cutter and use sugar paste to glue it on to the body.

2 Roll 15g (½oz) of brown paste into a ball then into a pear shape for the head. Make two holes for the eyes, two for the horns and two holes at the side of the head for the ears. Insert two white stamens for the eyes and using a black pen mark the pupils.

3 Make a muzzle by rolling out a small circle of white paste to fit over the end of the nose. Glue it in place.

4 Roll a small ball of white paste into a ball and cut it in two for nostrils. Roll both into small balls, then push one on to the rounded end of a pointed tool. Glue it in place on top of the muzzle and remove the tool, then repeat for the second nostril.

5 Mark the mouth with a circle cutter and use a pointed tool to make a hole at each end.

6 Roll 20g (⅔oz) of dark brown paste into a ball and cut it into four with scissors. Shape each piece as shown to make hooves, then use a palette knife to mark a line down the front of each one.

7 Roll 4g (⅛oz) of pale pink paste into a flat ball and push in four pink stamens to make an udder. Glue it in place at the bottom of the body.

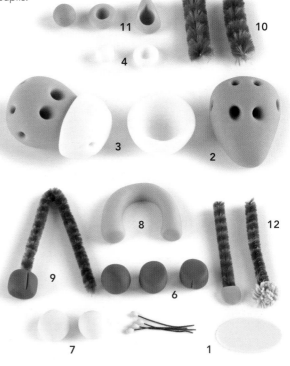

8 For the legs, roll out 17g (⁹⁄₁₆oz) of brown paste into a long smooth sausage. Use sugar glue to attach it in place half way around the body, then attach the hooves with sugar glue.

9 Cut a 15cm (6in) length of brown pipe cleaner, add glue and attach a hoof to each end. Bend the pipe cleaner round the back of the cocktail stick, glue it in place and bring the arms and hooves to the front.

10 Push the head on to the cocktail stick, using a little sugar glue. Next, cut two 3cm (1⅛in) lengths of pipe cleaner, and insert them into the top of the head along with a little glue to secure them.

11 For the ears, roll 5g (⅙oz) of brown paste into a ball. Cut it in half, roll each piece into a ball again, then push the round end of a

pointed tool into one ball. Without taking the tool out, add glue to the bottom part of the ear and place it on the side of the head over the hole. Pinch the top of the paste to make a pointed ear, then remove the tool and repeat with the other ear. Leave to dry.

12 Attach a small ball of paste to the end of a 7cm (2¾in) length of pipe cleaner to make the tail. Using the clay gun, make hair for the tail and the top of the head, then glue it in place. Push the tail in at the back of the body using a little glue.

13 Attach a bell on to the ribbon and tie it in place around the neck.

Sue
A quizzical cow is just the ticket for an animal-mad friend.

Blueberry Fairy

Materials:

100g (3½oz) purple modelling paste

35g (1¼oz) flesh coloured
  modelling paste

Small amount of white modelling paste

One purple pipe cleaner

Green stamens or sugar balls

Lilac royal icing

Purple glitter

Cocktail stick

Tools:

Basic tools (see page 7)

Thin palette knife

Cutters: medium blossom
  or carnation, small
  blossom, butterfly wing,
  tiny blossom

Small pair of scissors

Fine black fibre-tip pen

No. 2 icing nozzle and piping bag

Sugar glue

Rolling pin

Instructions:

1 Make a purple body as shown on page 6, then insert an 8cm (3¼in) cocktail stick. Make two holes in the front for the legs with the pointed tool.

2 Roll a 20g (⅔oz) ball of flesh coloured paste into a smooth ball for the head. Use a pointed tool to make a hole for the nose and use the smiley tool to mark the mouth.

3 Roll a small ball of flesh coloured paste into a cone for the nose. Using a little glue insert it into the hole. When the head is completely dry draw on the eyes using a fine fibre-tip black pen, or follow the instructions for the Sunflower Fairy (see page 20).

4 For the leg frills, roll out the purple paste and cut out two circles using a carnation cutter. Frill the edges then use a little sugar glue to secure them in place over the leg holes. Push the pointed tool though to remake the holes.

5 For the legs, cut a pipe cleaner in half and one piece in half again to make two 7.5cm (3in) leg lengths and one 15cm (6in) arm length.

6 Roll 12g (⁵⁄₁₂oz) of purple paste into a ball and cut it in half to make two oval shoes. Glue one end of a 7.5cm (3in) pipe cleaner and insert it into a shoe. Lightly glue the shoe and cover it with purple glitter, then shake off the excess. Add glue to the other end of the pipe cleaner and insert it into the body. Repeat with the other leg.

7 Roll 5g (⅙oz) of flesh coloured paste into a ball and cut it in half with the scissors to make two oval hands. Add a little sugar glue to each end of the pipe cleaner and attach the hands. Bend the pipe cleaner around the back of the cocktail stick and glue it in place, bringing the arms and hands down.

8 Roll out the white paste and use the medium size blossom cutter to cut out two neck frills. Soften the petal edges with the rounded end of the pointed tool. Add glue to the cocktail stick and place the frills on individually, pressing down firmly at the front and back. Push the head on to the cocktail stick using a little glue.

9 Cut out a butterfly wing from purple paste, lightly glue one side and cover it with glitter, before shaking off the excess. When dry, attach the wings to the back of the body with a little royal icing.

10 Use the piping bag with the no.2 icing nozzle to pipe small circles of pale lilac royal icing all over the head as hair.

11 Cut out two blossoms from white sugarpaste with the medium blossom cutter. Frill the edges with the rounded end of the pointed tool, then glue them on top of the head one at a time. Roll a small ball of purple paste and roll it gently to form a flattened ball. Lightly glue it on top of the blossoms then push in the green stamens. Alternatively, you can decorate it with green sugar balls.

12 Roll out small balls of lilac and purple sugarpaste for the baby blueberries and decorate each with a tiny white blossom secured with a green stamen. Leave to dry before marking the mouth and eyes with a pen.

Janet
I have so many children to look after, I think I have lost one!

Cat

Materials:

100g (3½oz) white modelling paste

Small amount of purple and lilac modelling paste

One purple pipe cleaner

Two white stamens

Ribbon (optional)

Cocktail stick

Pastry brush

Tools:

Basic tools (see page 7)

Cutters: large oval, tiny blossom

Thin palette knife

Small pair of scissors

Fine black fibre-tip pen

Small blossom cutter

Pastry brush

Sugar glue

Pin

Instructions:

1 Make a white body as shown on page 6 and insert an 8cm (3¼in) cocktail stick. Do not make any holes for the legs.

2 Using a small amount of purple paste and the large oval cutter, cut out an oval for the tummy and glue it in place.

3 Roll 20g (⅔oz) of white paste into a smooth ball for the head and shape it as shown. Support the head on a cocktail stick and use a pointed tool to make holes for the eyes. Insert the stamens and use a fine black fibre-tip pen to mark the pupils.

4 Roll 5g (⅙oz) of lilac paste into a ball, then gently roll it out to make a small thin oval shape for the muzzle. Glue it on to the face with sugar glue. Use a palette knife to mark three lines under the nose as shown to suggest the shape of the mouth.

5 Make a small cone of purple paste for the nose and insert it into the hole using a small amount of sugar glue.

6 Use scissors to cut a few bristles from a pastry brush. Push them into the cheeks on each side of the muzzle as whiskers. Trim, then use a pin to make a few small holes around the whiskers.

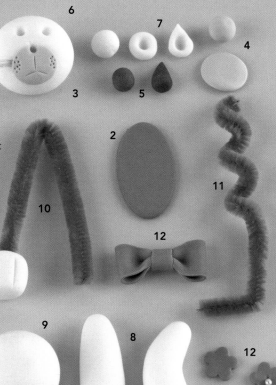

7 For the ears, roll 2g (¹⁄₁₂oz) of white paste into a ball and cut it in half. Roll each piece into a ball and push the rounded end of a pointed tool into one ball. Pinch the top of the paste to make a pointed ear, then add glue to the bottom part of the ear and place it on the top of the head firmly before removing the tool. Repeat with the other ear, then leave to dry.

8 For the legs, roll out 20g (²⁄₃oz) of white paste. Cut it in half and roll each half into a sausage to fit on either side of the body. Glue these legs in place and mark both as shown with a palette knife. Leave to dry.

9 Roll 15g (½oz) of white paste into a smooth ball and cut it in half for the paws. Roll each half into a ball and mark with a palette knife.

10 Cut a 15cm (6in) length of purple pipe cleaner for the arms. Add glue to each end and attach a paw. Bend the pipe cleaner round the back of the cocktail stick and glue it in place, bringing the arms and paws to the front.

11 Wrap the other half of the pipe cleaner around a pointed tool to make it into a curly tail. Using a little glue, push one end into the base of the body at the back.

12 Roll out purple sugarpaste and use the tiny blossom cutter to make a blossom. Secure this on the cat's head with a lilac stamen. Make a bow from the purple sugarpaste and glue it in place below the chin.

Claire

Have you seen my friends at the start and end of the book?

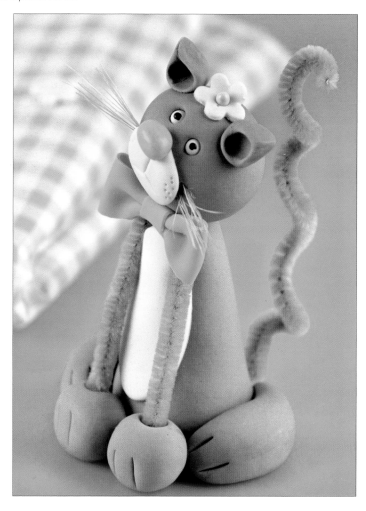

Acknowledgements

Special thanks to Edward, Marrianne, Debbie
and the rest of the team at Search Press for
all their hard work.

Publisher's Note

If you would like more information
about sugarcraft, try the following
books, all published by Search Press:
Twenty to Make Sugar Animals
Twenty to Make Sugar Birds
Twenty to Make Sugar Fairies
Sensational Sugar Animals
Mini Sugar Shoes